Bungalo Books

SNOW

JOHN BIANCHI & FRANK B. EDWARDS

W9-ABF-671

LEARNING FOR THE FUN OF IT

Written by Frank B. Edwards
Illustrated by John Bianchi
Copyright 1992 by Bungalo Books

Canadian Cataloguing in Publication Data

Edwards, Frank B., 1952-
    Snow: learning for the fun of it

ISBN 0-921285-15-9 (bound)
ISBN 0-921285-09-4 (pbk.)

1. Snow — Juvenile literature
I. Bianchi, John
II. Title.

QH926.37.E49 1992   j551.57'84   C92-090405-X

Published in Canada by:
Bungalo Books
Box 129
Newburgh, Ontario
KOK 2S0

Co-published in U.S.A. by:
Firefly Books (U.S.) Inc.
Ellicott Station
P.O. Box 1338
Buffalo, New York
14205

Trade distribution by:
Firefly Books Ltd.
250 Sparks Avenue
Willowdale, Ontario
M2H 2S4

Designed by:
Jonathan Robert Bungalo & Associates

Printed in Canada by:
Friesen Printers
Altona, Manitoba

Film preparation by:
Hadwen Graphics
Ottawa, Ontario

When we set out to write this book, all we knew about snow was that it was cold and wet and that it fell on us every winter. While we played in it, skied on it and occasionally got hit in the head with it, we weren't sure we could write an interesting book about it.

Our researcher, Laurel Aziz, changed our minds. After several months of gathering material, she dumped a few thousand pages of information about snow on our desks. By the time we finished reading it all, we had learned more about snow than we had ever thought possible. But most important, we had discovered new ways of looking at a familiar subject.

We hope this book will help you find new ways to look at snow as well. And when you are finished thinking about snow, maybe you will find something else that also deserves a closer look — just for the fun of it.

Frank B. Edwards & John Bianchi

SNOWFLAKES UP CLOSE

Many people claim that no two snowflakes look exactly alike — a popular belief that probably dates back to the observations of an eccentric Vermont farmer who photographed over 5,000 snowflakes early in the 20th century. Considering that billions and billions of individual flakes fall during a single storm, it is probably safer to say that no person has ever seen two identical snowflakes before. It may also be safe to say that very few people spend much time looking for ones that match.

Snowflakes, of course, do come in many different shapes and sizes, but no matter what they look like at nose level, they all start out as tiny ice crystals floating about in a cloud. They acquire their final shape during their long journey from the cloud in which they are born to earth.

Snowflakes are the result of an amazing chain reaction that takes place when the water vapour in a cloud reaches a supercool temperature and then starts to bump into the tiny dust particles which clouds usually carry. The dust particle may be a speck of dirt blown into the air from a dry field or a grain of pollen from a flower, but when it meets cold water vapour, it wraps a water molecule around itself, changing the molecule from vapour to an ice crystal (in a process called *sublimation*).

This ice crystal then grows larger by bumping into and sticking to other vapour molecules. After about an hour of circulating through the cloud gathering more water molecules, the ice crystal is the size of a raindrop and becomes heavy enough to begin its descent to earth. On its way down, it may collide and join with other ice crystals to form a complex snowflake. In fact, a single fluffy snowflake may consist of hundreds of tiny ice crystals. The largest flake ever recorded was 10 centimetres (4 in.), the diameter of a regular-sized hamburger bun.

To make their work easier, scientists have set up a system that classifies snowflakes by their seven basic shapes.

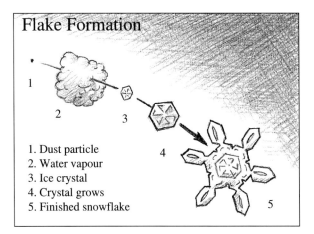

Flake Formation

1. Dust particle
2. Water vapour
3. Ice crystal
4. Crystal grows
5. Finished snowflake

Hexagonal (six-sided) plates form at mild temperatures of 0 to minus 25 degrees C (32°-9°F). Due to their delicate nature, they grow large only in still air and may combine with stellar crystals to form complex snowflakes.

Hexagonal Plate

Stellar Crystal

Stellar (or star) crystals can grow almost to the size of a penny. They form in moderately cold clouds of minus 10 to minus 20 degrees C (24°-14°F), usually in windless weather (rough weather would damage their arms).

Spatial Dendrite

While stellar crystals are flat and symmetrical, spatial dendrites have an irregular shape, with arms (known as *dendrites*) sticking out of their side branches. They are formed in large, moisture-laden clouds.

Irregular crystals are the most common form of snow, occurring in turbulent weather when a crystal cannot drift through a cloud slowly enough to grow in an orderly fashion. They form in moderately cold clouds.

Irregular Crystal

Needles

Needles are hexagonal shafts about the size of rice grains that are common in moderately cold weather. Needles can combine with one another but do not fall with other crystal types. Lightning may accompany the snow.

Columns

Columns are small hexagonal shafts that form in cold temperatures below minus 22 degrees C (–12°F). They occur in high wispy clouds and can create haloes in the sky as light passes through their prisms.

When columns form in the high end of their temperature range, they may collide with hexagonal plates, adding caps to their ends and even their middles. Capped columns are much larger than plain columns.

Capped Column

A life in the snow

Wilson A. Bentley, an eccentric bachelor from Jericho, Vermont, photographed 5,300 snowflakes over 46 winters. He became fascinated by snow as a young man, and despite a lack of formal education, he eventually gave up farming to pursue his snowflake studies. He became famous for a book with over 3,000 black-and-white pictures of snowflakes; it proved valuable to scientists classifying snowflake shapes, but because Bentley had altered many of his photos to make the flakes look more attractive, it had limited scientific use. He died of pneumonia on Christmas Eve in 1931 at the age of 68.

CLICK!

Snowflakes on the Move

Glaciers are just about the largest and most destructive moving objects on Earth. It is hard to believe that they are made of snowflakes.

When new snowflakes land on top of old ones, the old ones are crushed against their neighbours. If the sun melts the snow during the day, the moisture that flows between the flakes refreezes at night, binding individual snowflakes together. Gradually, the snow is packed into ice.

In our backyards, all of the winter's snow melts away each spring. But in very cold areas, each year's new snow lies on top of the old snow, and the snowdrifts just keep getting deeper. As the buried snow turns to ice over hundreds of years, a glacier is born.

Today, thousands of glaciers dot our planet, covering 10 percent of the surface. The largest and oldest are in the Antarctic: almost 4.5 kilometres (3 mi.) thick, they have been growing for the past 15 million years.

Many glaciers form in mountains, and as they grow bigger, their weight forces them to move downhill, carving out huge valleys as they go. Anything that gets in their way either is pushed along in front of the advancing glacier or slips underneath it. Usually, glaciers move forward very slowly, but every so often, a glacier will surge forward, moving several kilometres in a matter of months. While a few villages have been destroyed by glaciers over the past 1,000 years, no modern city has been threatened yet.

Massive destruction by glaciers generally occurs only during ice ages, and the last ice age ended about 12,000 years ago, back in a primitive time before humans had learned to build houses. However, when the next ice age occurs, the glaciers' victims will certainly include the cities that were built in their path. Luckily for us, that will be thousands of years from now.

9

How Glaciers Work

Even though they are made of snow and ice, glaciers are incredibly powerful. Like many superheroes, they appear to be mild-mannered until they swing into action. Then nothing can stop them.

As a glacier advances, the accumulated rubble acts like a crude file, scraping away the earth to bare bedrock. It leaves deep scars wherever it goes and can actually gouge out valleys and lakes in soft bedrock. When ice sheets covered most of Canada and the northern United States 10,000 years ago, the sheer weight of the ice flattened much of the continent, leaving behind huge level plains throughout the West.

Farther east, the ice sheet gouged out troughs that became the Great Lakes. On the northern coasts of the Pacific and Atlantic oceans, glaciers carved deep valleys on their way to the sea. When the ice finally melted away, unblocking the mouths of these coastal valleys, seawater flooded into them, creating deep fjords with high, steep walls.

Glaciers are so large, it is hard to imagine them moving. In fact, they don't really move along the ground the way a car travels; they simply grow in size as snow accumulates on top of them. As they grow taller and heavier, their weight pushes downward and forces their edges outward, so they appear to be moving. Rocks and soil are pushed ahead of the advancing ice, creating gigantic piles of debris called moraines that eventually become gently rolling hills.

Glaciers stop moving when warm temperatures prevent their growth. As they slowly shrink, their edges stop advancing and begin to melt away. Icy cold water rushes out from underneath, filling the holes the glacier has left. As the glacier's ice melts, it leaves behind clues to its travels: narrow lakes fill its deep scratches in bedrock, long rows of hills show the extent of its advance, huge erratic boulders sit where the melting ice left them, and wide valleys mark where glaciers squeezed between two mountains.

Icebergs

When the front of a slow-moving glacier reaches an ocean coast, large parts of it break off and fall into the water, creating icebergs that float away in whichever direction the current pushes them.

Each year, about 10,000 to 15,000 icebergs crash noisily into the Arctic Ocean from glaciers in Greenland and Canada. Most of these icebergs melt away in approximately two years, and only about 400 a year actually find their way south into the Atlantic Ocean. (One of them sank the *Titanic* in 1912, killing 1,513 passengers.)

However, some of the really big ones have been known to travel as far south as Bermuda. As they slowly disintegrate, icebergs leave a trail of smaller piano-sized pieces called *growlers* and *bergy bits* the size of houses.

The Antarctic dumps a trillion tonnes of ice into the ocean each year. Its icebergs are much larger — up to eight kilometres (5 mi.) long and 15 storeys tall — and can last for 10 years. The largest on record, spotted in 1956, was half the size of Prince Edward Island.

Where did these rocks come from?

The mountain valleys of Switzerland are littered with 18,000-tonne granite boulders as big as houses. For centuries, people believed that these rocks (which were worn and smooth) had been washed down from nearby mountains during the flood described in the Bible story of Noah's Ark.

In the 1750s, however, a few daring scientists suggested that the rocks had been dragged along the valleys by mountain glaciers many kilometres away. But people refused to believe that huge glaciers could move such a distance, let alone litter the ground with gigantic rocks.

In 1837, Louis Agassiz, a Swiss fossil expert, went even further, declaring that all of Europe had once been covered by an enormous sheet of ice that had moved back and forth — dropping boulders and carving new features into the continent. People were outraged and attacked his theories for years. But Agassiz continued to explore Europe and North America, finding evidence of glacial changes everywhere. By the time he died in 1873, the world had finally begun to accept that ancient ice ages had indeed existed and that they had changed the shape of the world.

THE LAST AGE OF SNOW

Eighteen thousand years ago, one-third of the Earth's surface was covered by gigantic sheets of ice over 1.6 kilometres (1 mi.) thick. The planet was locked in an ice age — caused by a fluke of nature in which the snow did not melt in summer. The Arctic snow fell for a few thousand years, forming ice sheets that eventually covered Canada and much of the northern United States.

As the ice moved slowly forward, it swept up everything in its path, flattening the land and scooping up entire forests — trees, rocks and soil. This particular ice age, named the Wisconsin, was the world's last and started 35,000 years ago. With each winter's snowfall, the mighty ice sheets grew larger and larger, advancing for about 17,000 years. When they reached the coasts, chunks of them broke off into huge icebergs that floated away, cooling the oceans as they melted.

Winds that blew across these continental ice sheets carried cold air around the world, slowly changing the planet. In many parts of the world, plants that needed a warm climate died out, to be replaced by smaller, hardier species. Even forests untouched by ice died, as cold weather permanently froze the ground in which they grew. Some animals migrated away from the cold, while others adapted to it. North America was filled with an amazing assortment of hardy animals: woolly mammoths with long tusks, huge beavers, bears the size of moose and giant sabre-toothed cats.

Gradually, the climate began to warm up, and the glaciers started to melt. For 8,000 years, their cold waters fuelled huge floods, leaving vast lakes behind where the ice had once been. The land, already shaped by ice, was reshaped by water.

By the time the ice and water were gone, some parts of the world had changed completely — several times. Much of America's forest had been replaced by lush grasslands, and many of the animals that had thrived in the shadow of the ice had disappeared forever — including the woolly mammoth.

When Snow Won't Go Away

For the past two million years, Earth has had a serious problem with ice and snow. While it was a tropical paradise before the current Quaternary period started, our planet has suffered through about 20 ice ages since. For 60,000 to 90,000 years at a time, glaciers spread out and destroyed everything in their path; then they melted away over the next 10,000 to 40,000 years, flooding the land they crushed.

Before our last ice age ended roughly 12,000 years ago, about one-third of the Earth's surface was under ice. Even now, glaciers cover nearly 10 percent of the planet, mostly at the North and South poles. It is not surprising that Earth was much different then. Oddly enough, the average annual temperatures were only a few degrees cooler than they are today; winters were long but relatively mild, while summers were short and cold. Winds, caused by the temperature difference between

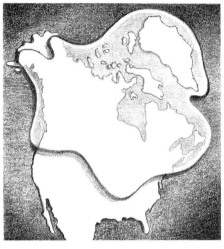

the cold glaciers and the unfrozen ground, were a serious problem. While today's winds pick up moisture for rain from lakes, the winds blowing across the ice were dry — and very cold. In fact, fierce winds raged most of the time, and because the ground was so dry, there were dust storms that lasted for years.

When ocean winds dropped their moisture, it was often in the form of snow, which simply made the glaciers bigger. Because that moisture became locked in ice, the oceans began to shrink. As the ice grew higher, the ocean levels sank lower. Eventually, some parts of the seafloor were exposed — a land bridge that emerged between Asia and Alaska provided early tribes of people (and many animal species) with a route to North America.

The presence of so much ice meant the land was constantly changing. Not only did the ice scrape away everything in its path, but its incredible weight flattened everything under it. Even the land that was not touched by ice was altered just by the cold. Forests died out because of the cold and the high winds, and fertile land was replaced by permafrost, ground that was always frozen.

When the glaciers melted, their waters flooded the land, filling the depressions and holes the ice had left. Huge seas covered much of North America for a few thousand years before they finally drained into the ocean, gradually restoring the sea level of the world again.

In the end, when the ice and water had gone, the ground looked like a vacant lot after a bulldozer has levelled all the trees. But it wasn't long before seeds blew in and plants began to grow. Grasses did well on the prairies, which had been covered with deep deposits of rich, windblown soil, while forests grew elsewhere. With the weight of the ice and water gone, the landscape rose in many places. Today, everywhere you look, there are clues to the effects of the ice age, from hilly ridges to river valleys and lakes.

Warmer Weather Spelled Extinction

The woolly mammoth was an animal well suited to the long, cold winters and short summers of ice ages. With its warm, shaggy coat, it had a good defence against the bitter winds that blew constantly, and as a grazer, it fed on the grasses which grew where other plants could not. Mammoths thrived in North America for 1.5 million years but went extinct about 12,000 years ago, near the end of the last ice age. Scientists guess that migrating tribes of Clovis people, crossing the land bridge from Asia to Alaska 20,000 years ago, may have hunted mammoths to extinction or that the warming of the climate ruined the rich grasslands — either by flooding or by the invasion of unsuitable plants and trees. Altogether, 40 large North American mammals became extinct at the end of the last ice age, and the exact reason remains a mystery.

Predicting a warm-weather ice age

Today, people worry more about the gradual warming of the Earth's climate than the arrival of the next ice age. But climatologist Hermann Flohn predicts that warmer weather could, in fact, trigger another ice age.

As cars and industries pollute the air, the atmosphere becomes clogged with carbon dioxide, which acts like a giant blanket of insulation. Heat cannot escape into space, and this greenhouse effect raises the world's temperature.

Flohn's *snowblitz* theory predicts that as temperatures rise, the world's glaciers will start to melt, adding fresh water to the oceans. As the ocean level rises by 5 to 50 metres (15-150 ft.), the huge Antarctic ice sheet that now rests on top of an underwater mountain range will float free and slip into the ocean. This massive iceberg will cool the world's oceans by several degrees, possibly even freezing them as their salt content is diluted. Winds blowing across the ice will cause blizzards that will feed new glaciers. Eventually, the cold temperatures generated by this ice will overpower the warmth of the greenhouse effect, and Earth will become locked in another ice age.

A COLD BLAST OF WINTER

Blizzards are snowstorms that have gone wild. Low temperatures and high winds combined with heavy snowfall create howling storms that can bury the countryside in snow. Even after the snowflakes stop falling, the wind whips the fallen snow off the ground and back into the air, blowing it into huge drifts whenever its pathway is blocked. There is so much blowing snow that people cannot see where they are going.

German settlers experiencing their first winter in Iowa during the 19th century coined the word blizzard from the German phrase for "lightning-like." Coming from a much more moderate climate, the settlers were surprised by the speed and intensity with which these storms struck.

One of the worst blizzards in recent times hit western New York State and southern Ontario in late January of 1977. High winds and heavy snowfall covered the area in giant drifts that were often higher than telephone lines. The city of Buffalo and its one million residents came to a standstill: all schools were closed for a week, and some children were trapped at school for three days. The storm descended on the city so quickly that the streets filled with snow before many people had a chance to get home safely. Over 13,000 people had to spend the night wherever they were. Shoppers slept in stores, while workers stayed in offices and factories.

The greatest danger during a blizzard is the bitterly cold temperatures. Today, most homes are well heated and stocked with groceries, but the pioneers risked death if they ran out of firewood and food before the blizzard ended. Even a trip outside for fuel or drinking water was dangerous, because blowing snow could disorient people, and then they would be unable to find their way back to the house.

Mixing Good Weather With Bad

North America is a huge mixing bowl of weather in which cold, dry air from the Arctic regions of Canada is blended with warm, moist air from the Gulf of Mexico, as well as the Atlantic and Pacific oceans. Depending on the mix, the final weather can range from cool, clear skies to thunderstorms, cyclones and blizzards.

Each winter, the prairies are hit by at least one major blizzard, usually the result of strong, frigid winds that roar down from the North, dumping fine-grained snow along their path. The cold weather these *northers* leave behind often mixes with moist air coming over the Rockies and creates another kind of blizzard that adds strong southeasterly winds and even more snow.

In mid-March 1888, just such a moist low-pressure trough of air swept eastward across the United States, depositing snow along the Canadian border and pushing cyclones through Georgia. While meteorologists predicted that the cyclones would exhaust themselves over the Atlantic, they were surprised when one of them returned to the mainland near New York City. As the low-pressure trough approached the eastern coast, cold air from Newfoundland rushed in to meet it, and one of the worst blizzards in people's memory was born.

Weather in the area turned bitterly cold overnight, and the wind howled for two days, dropping snow knee-deep and then whipping it into high drifts that blocked doors and windows. Prairie farmers were used to such bad weather, but New Yorkers were stunned. Many of them died trying to get through the streets, collapsing exhausted into snowdrifts and freezing to death. Trains could not run, telegraph lines snapped, stores closed, and people went hungry. After the storm, thousands of men, working for 30 cents an hour, began to clear the streets and tracks. A few days later, warm weather finished the job.

The Blizzards of 1888 and 1977

New York City, March 1888

✳ more than 400 people die of accident or cold

✳ 198 ships sink or are damaged; hundreds of trains are stuck; horses are unable to travel

✳ 50,000 New Yorkers are kept from work

✳ telegraph service is cut off between New York, Washington, Boston and Philadelphia

✳ newspapers publish but cannot reach readers

✳ thousands of people are hired to shovel snow by hand (30¢/hr.); some rural residents in New England are snowed in for two weeks

Western New York State, February 1977

✳ 28 people die of accident or cold

✳ air travel is restricted for a week; thousands of cars and trucks are abandoned on highways

✳ more than 750,000 workers are stuck at home

✳ 1.2 million long-distance calls are made in Buffalo area on first day of blizzard

✳ newspapers publish but cannot reach readers; TV and radio broadcast constant storm updates

✳ 300 people clear Buffalo sidewalks ($3.88/hr.); snowploughs are borrowed from other cities

Surviving the fury of a storm

When the blizzard of 1977 hit Ontario, 9-year-old Tonya Plummer was on a snowmobile trip with her father and two friends near their cottage north of Toronto. Starting out to visit a nearby island in clear weather, they were caught off guard by the sudden storm. High winds engulfed them in swirling snow, and they could not see where they were going. They sought shelter on an uninhabited island. Worried about becoming lost and freezing to death, the foursome dug a large hole in the side of a snowdrift and climbed into it. They built a fire in front of the shelter to help keep them warm, because the high winds and cold temperatures made it feel as if it was minus 40 degrees C (–40°F). Even though they had no food, they were able to melt snow for drinking water. Luckily, they were warmly dressed, and Tonya had an extra pair of socks to share, although she burned a hole in her mitts while tending the fire. The storm died down after three days, and they were rescued by a police helicopter. Tonya had frostbitten fingers but was fine after two days in hospital.

Travelling over snow

European explorers arriving in Canada in the 1500s quickly realized that snow posed a serious problem for them. They were not used to the severe winters of the New World and had little experience travelling in snow. Unlike their British counterparts, the French proved quite willing to take the advice of the native people and adopted the Algonquins' snowshoe for their own use.

The snowshoe was an ingenious device with leather lacing on a hardwood frame shaped like a huge bear paw. Strapped to a moccasin, it spread the weight of a human over a wide area and prevented a person from sinking into deep snow. Equipped with snowshoes, people could walk on top of the snow, instead of floundering about with each step. Fur traders found them essential, and even the soldiers of New France used them.

The English were much less adaptable and refused to stoop to such primitive technology until midway through the 18th century, during their colonial war with France. Forced into winter battles in the rugged countryside of Quebec and New York, British generals finally agreed that snowshoes were necessary if their armies were to outmanoeuvre the French.

Snowshoes were not as novel an item as these newcomers thought. While the Algonquins and other native groups had created their own designs, the snowshoe seems to have been in use since 4000 B.C. in central Asia. No doubt it eased the advance of early Asian tribes into northern Europe.

As the colonies expanded and early settlements grew into towns and cities, snowshoeing became a popular pastime in both Canada and the United States. Military clubs started the trend, but by the 1840s, there were active snowshoe organizations for men and women throughout Quebec and New England. Although skis were introduced to Montreal in 1895 by a Norwegian, they were considered clumsy and difficult. They finally became popular in the 1930s, just as mechanics were experimenting with motorized snow machines.

A History of Staying on Top of the Snow

Several thousand years ago, humans living in snowy areas of the world realized they could imitate the animals that walked on top of the snow instead of breaking through the crust with each step. By "increasing" the size of their feet on the snow — either with snowshoes or skis — people were able to expend much less energy travelling. Skis were used in Scandinavia from about 3000 B.C., making them a somewhat more recent invention than snowshoes. A cave drawing in Norway indicates the use of a single long pole for balance, suggesting that early skiers probably shuffled along fairly slowly compared with the pace of modern cross-country racers.

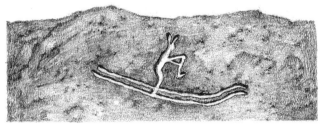

Sleds were developed about 2,000 years before skis, no doubt a logical solution to the problem of balancing a load while falling through knee-deep snow. Although Inuit found that sleds with runners worked well on the shallow snow in the Arctic, wide, flat-bottomed toboggans were the choice of people who had to cope with deeper snow.

For a long time, snow proved to be a serious obstacle to people trying to exploit the resources of North America, but gradually they began to adapt technology to snow travel. After European miners brought skis to the mountains of California during the 1849 gold rush, their popularity spread all the way to Alaska and the Yukon.

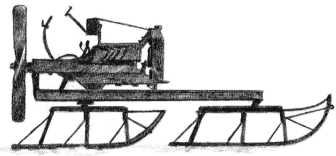

But it was the invention of the gasoline engine that really eased travel through the snowy regions of the world. In 1922, Armand Bombardier put a car engine and a huge propeller on some old sleigh runners and invented the first snowmobile. It looked like a wingless airplane but eventually evolved into a tracked vehicle that could travel anywhere across deep snow and ice. Bombardier and others went on to build snow vehicles that could move people and equipment long distances at high speeds. The days of the fur traders' sleds and snowshoes were long over; soon, mining and forestry companies were going into areas that had been inaccessible earlier in the century.

Today, many isolated parts of Canada rely on snow to provide a surface for winter travel. Once the early snows are packed down to form temporary roads, villages and mine sites surrounded by wet muskeg can have supplies brought in all winter by trucks with huge balloon tires.

Dog Versus Machine

While most aboriginal people in North America pulled sleds through snow themselves, Inuit of the North put dogs to work for them centuries ago. Using teams of dogs, Inuit could haul loads of half a tonne 100 kilometres (60 mi.) in a day over snow-covered terrain that would be difficult to walk across. This was important in a land where game could be many days' travel away from villages.

The dogs were also useful in the hunt itself, tracking seals and chasing polar bears, and in times of emergency, they could be eaten. Dogs were not perfect companions, however, requiring a large helping of fish each day that had to be either carried in the sled or caught fresh.

When Armand Bombardier brought his first snowmobile (called a Ski-Dog) to the North in 1952, trappers welcomed it as an alternative to dog teams. By 1959, they could buy his Skidoos, which travelled 40 kilometres per hour (24 mph) and used only gasoline and oil. Within a decade, the machines were more common than dog teams, and Bombardier was selling 15,000 a year.

Champion snow musher

The Iditarod is the world's longest and richest sled-dog race. Set in Alaska, it runs from Anchorage to Nome — a distance of 1,872 kilometres (1,163 mi.). Each March, dog teams brave cold temperatures, wilderness trails and snowstorms to compete for a $50,000 grand prize.

The race was established in 1973 to preserve the memory of the husky dogs that were once the most important form of transportation in the North. It is a tough and dangerous race that tests the endurance and courage of both the dogs and their drivers.

One of the most successful racers is Susan Butcher, a dog lover from Massachusetts who moved to Alaska in 1975 at age 20 to become a sled-dog racer. After several tries, she won the Iditarod for the first time in 1983, setting a new record time of 11 days 15 hours and 6 minutes.

The owner of more than 50 dogs, Butcher trains her team on practice runs of up to 100 kilometres (60 mi.). She has dedicated her life to dogs and sledding, proving her skills with four Iditarod wins.

COPING WITH SNOW

When automobiles made their first appearance around 1900, winter travel was not considered possible. The cars were primitive, and no one expected much of them. But by 1919, when there were tens of thousands of cars, the most progressive municipalities began to plough snow from the roads regularly.

Today, large cities spend huge amounts of money on snow removal. Montreal, Canada's snowiest big city, gets about 40 snowstorms a year, which cost more than $60 million a winter to clean up. Each year, 350,000 dump-truck loads of snow are hauled from its 2,000 kilometres (1,200 mi.) of streets so that people can go about their business despite the weather.

The workhorse of snow removal is a dump truck fitted with a large blade on the front and a wing on the side. Pushed at a steady speed, the plough eases snow into the path of the wing, which throws it clear of the road.

To manage the huge task of keeping snow off its streets, Montreal has about 2,000 workers and 1,600 removal vehicles that clear specific routes during each snowstorm. When snow starts to fall, an army of trucks is dispatched to spread a mixture of salt, crushed stone and sand onto the streets. The salt mix not only melts the snow and ice but also gives car wheels traction so that they do not skid. Many cities can clear much of their annual snowfall by simply melting it in the streets.

But if a storm continues and snow starts to collect, ploughs are sent out. Generally, main streets receive top priority, as they carry the most traffic across the city. In Montreal, crews try to clear all streets within 72 hours of a storm.

Simply pushing snow off the road until it melts is fine in the country, but in the city, ploughs are followed by snow blowers that scoop up the snow and blast it into trucks to be dumped into nearby rivers or vacant snow dumps. Some cities have trucks with large melting units on them that melt the piles of snow beside the streets, flushing the waste-water into nearby storm sewers.

Paving the Streets With Snow

The practice of shovelling snow off roads in winter is less than 100 years old. In the last century, people depended on snow-covered roads to make their travels safer and more comfortable. In fact, until railroads were built between cities, many people waited until winter to do their long-distance travelling.

Early roads in both Canada and the United States were little more than trails through the woods. As land was divided up and given to settlers, surveyors marked roadways, but it was often left to the newly arrived pioneers to make the roads for their communities by cutting down trees and removing the stumps. Even after that was done, the road was a mess of holes and bumps and could be swamped with mud and water after each rain.

Winter, however, brought enough snow to cover the primitive pathways. After a few runs over it, fresh snow was packed down enough to give travellers a smooth ride. With the first good snowfall each November, the rickety stagecoaches and wagons that travelled between towns were replaced by sleighs on runners, which were much faster and glided over the surface. Snow was not a perfect road covering, because warm weather would melt it occasionally, leading to horrendous shaking and grinding whenever the sleigh hit a patch of bare gravel or rock, but generally, people liked winter roads. Wrapped snugly in blankets and buffalo robes, they could stay warm for short jaunts, while long-distance travellers hoped that their stagecoach would be a modern one equipped with a small wood stove.

While snow was a serious problem for travellers in mountain regions, where avalanches could block passes for days or weeks, it was usually considered an ally — until the advent of trains. Despite their weight and speed, locomotives could not travel through deep snow, so the first snowploughs were designed for trains, and crews were kept busy each winter clearing snow from bridges, switches and tracks.

Organized snow removal from streets became common in cities only after streetcar tracks were built. Until then, sidewalks were kept clear by homeowners and storekeepers: the snow was shovelled into the streets, the piles getting higher with each snowfall. By the end of winter, the roadways for horse-drawn sleighs were far above the sidewalk level, and spring thaws often brought floods.

The growth of streetcar tracks in the 1880s forced an end to this practice in the cities, and by the 1920s, governments were regularly removing snow from their newly built highways to keep car and truck owners happy.

Road Warriors

In 1881, a dispute between a streetcar company and city residents almost turned into a riot on Toronto's main street. Employees of the Street Railway Company were clearing the tracks of their horse-drawn streetcars by throwing the snow onto the sidewalk after a heavy snowfall. Business owners, worried that customers could not get into their stores, started shovelling it back onto the tracks. Snow throwing led to hostile words, which escalated to fistfights. When the brawl ended, the streetcars were left stuck in the snow.

Snow That Pollutes

After a heavy snowfall, city crews must clear the snow from the streets by trucking it away. Some cities maintain huge yards where they pile up snow so that it can melt in spring, while others simply dump it into nearby rivers. This leads to new problems of pollution, because snow that has lain on streets is filled with such harmful chemicals as lead (from car exhaust), oil, salt, zinc and phosphorus. When the snow melts, concentrated amounts of these pollutants end up in rivers, groundwater and soil.

The first shovel

Ever since people made their way into the northern parts of the world 200,000 years ago, they have had to deal with snow. Once prehistoric people recognized snowdrifts as a problem, they had to figure out how to move them and then invent an appropriate tool. Archaeological evidence suggests that the earliest shovels date back about 6,000 years and were made of locally available materials. A primitive shovel blade discovered in a Russian peat bog is made of an oval section of elk antler about the size of a sheet of notebook paper. Six small holes in it indicate that it was tied to a stick or bone handle to give the user leverage to lift it easily. It was too thin for heavy work, but scientists think it was used to shovel snow or loose soil.

FUN IN THE SNOW

A heavy snowfall generally causes all sorts of problems, mostly related to travel. It blocks roads, slows traffic, creates slippery conditions that lead to accidents and just makes a real mess of everything from big-city rush hours to airline schedules. Yet snow does not mean bad news for everyone. Over the last 100 years, changes in technology and family life have finally given us the chance to have fun in the snow.

The advances of the 20th century include regular holidays and weekend breaks from school and work. Not only do people have more time to play in winter, but they also have warmer clothing and a wide assortment of toys.

Many snow toys have been fashioned from the tools adults once used to cope with snow. The toboggan is an obvious example. After centuries of use by natives and fur traders, it was replaced by motorized vehicles. But instead of disappearing completely, the toboggan and the European-style sled took on new roles as toys. In place of the supplies they previously held, they now carry screaming kids — and the occasional terrified parent.

Skiing started as a method for hunters to get food during winter. When the Norwegian Army adopted skis in 1716, it led to such contests as the biathlon, which blends shooting and racing. The sport took a new direction in 1879, when 10,000 Norwegians attended the first national ski-jumping competition — skiers descended hills at high speed and hit bumps that jolted them into the air. Jumping enthusiasts later tried out the mountains of Europe and set the stage for Alpine skiing.

Not all snow toys came from adult tools, though. The first snowmobile was built in 1922 by a 15-year-old Quebecker, Armand Bombardier, who was simply interested in creating a machine that would carry him across the snow. He later developed dozens of large tracked vehicles but eventually returned to his original idea of a small snowmobile that could be used for transportation, recreation and racing.

Going Downhill

Playing in snow 100 years ago was much different than it is now. Clothing was not as warm as today's insulated snowsuits, and boots were made of leather, which could not keep feet dry. While children did play outside on snowy, cold days, they were hampered by heavy, bulky clothing that made it difficult to move. It was hard to have fun when faced with cold temperatures and wet snow. Given a choice between a snowdrift and a warm spot near a kitchen cookstove, many children chose to play indoors much of the winter.

Snowshoeing was probably the favourite winter activity in 19th-century North America. Families in snowy places like Montreal and the New England States often went on Sunday outings, travelling to parks (such as Montreal's Mont-Royal) if they lived in towns or to neighbouring farms if they were in the country. Snowshoe clubs were organized in cities throughout the eastern snowbelt regions.

Skiing did not become popular in these areas until at least the 1920s. Up until the 1870s, skis were found mainly in Norway, where they had been a common mode of transportation for centuries. There were occasional cross-country races there, but skiing did not become a widespread sport until 1879, when Norway held its first national ski-jumping contest. As ski jumping became more common, it spread to the Alps in central Europe, and by 1900, people were skiing downhill just for the fun of it. Over the next 20 years, ski clubs began to outnumber snowshoe clubs, competitions sprang up everywhere, and experienced skiers started their own ski schools.

As skiing became more widespread, people started to demand international competitions. Finally, in 1924, the International Olympic Committee sponsored the first Winter Olympics in Chamonix, France. They included skating events as well as ski jumping and cross-country races. While the Scandinavian countries worried that the new winter games would hurt their own competitions, the biggest problem faced by organizers has always been snow — or, rather, a continuing lack of it. Warm weather and rain have plagued many of the games over the years: truckloads of snow had to be shipped to Lake Placid, New York, from Canada in 1932, and the Calgary Olympics in 1988 suffered from warm chinook winds that melted bobsled tracks and ski runs.

Alpine (downhill) skiing for pleasure became a popular pastime in North America during the 1950s and 1960s, a time when higher family incomes meant more money for equipment and travel. Today, there are over 1,000 ski resorts in North America and endless ski trails.

Modern synthetic ski clothing has been designed to keep the body warm and dry without restricting movement. And this, more than anything, has

The Perfect Packing Snow

The art of the perfect snowball certainly demands some manual dexterity, but the quality of snow is actually far more important than the physical skill required to scoop up a mound of snow with two hands and pat it into shape.

Fresh snowflakes, especially those that fall in very cold weather, usually contain 20 times more air than ice crystals and do not make good snowballs. Packing a mound of snow with your hands will compact the individual crystals and remove the extra air, but it will not bind them together.

A good snowball needs crystals which stick together, and water molecules provide the glue. Even in cold weather, the sun melts the top layers of snow, and as water drips deeper into a drift, it covers the lower crystals with a wet coating that binds the frozen water molecules to one another. In cold weather, there is less such melting and snowballs are light and dry, while warmer temperatures produce heavier, wetter snowballs.

The deadly snowball fight

San Francisco, California, seldom gets any snow, but when a snowstorm hit in 1887, the children of the city went wild. Kids who had never seen snow before instinctively knew how to make snowballs, and snow battles raged throughout the city. Some adults, however, did not appreciate the new sport at all.

One man named Thomas Shine was attacked by three boys who had been throwing snowballs at passersby all day. Not realizing that snow fights were supposed to be fun, he became angry, pulled out a self-cocking bulldog revolver and fired four shots. Luckily, his aim was poor, and he missed each time, scaring the boys away. A passing police officer arrested him for assault with a deadly weapon. The boys were not charged, although other people who accidentally broke windows with snowballs were arrested for mischief.

PEOPLE OF THE SNOW

When the prehistoric Clovis hunters of the last ice age crossed the land bridge to Alaska about 20,000 years ago, they headed south, leaving no civilization behind. But the next wave of migrants chose to stay, struggling to adapt to the harsh climate.

These new people, now known as the Arctic Small Tools people, arrived about 2300 B.C. and were named for the simple artifacts they left behind. There is little explanation of why they came, but their constant search for animals took them all across the Arctic region.

From this original group, a subculture called the Dorset people evolved in the eastern Arctic. Amazingly, they survived for about 3,000 years, using the sparse materials the barren land offered them. Before their eventual disappearance, about 1000 A.D., they developed two crucial devices: the sled and the igloo. The sleds were made of bones and hides, with frozen fish wrapped in skins for runners. The igloos were built of snow.

These were important inventions in a land with few building materials. Although they were simple ideas, they were so effective that the more advanced Thule people who arrived from Asia about 1000 A.D. adopted them too.

The Thules originally settled on the Alaskan coast, where they lived in houses of driftwood, animal bones and skins and used seaworthy boats to hunt whales. But as they spread eastward to hunt, they needed to develop new skills to survive the colder climate. Their introduction to the ways of the Dorset tribes (who by then were dying out) gave them the igloo and sled, which they added to their boats, kayaks, oil lamps, knives and more sophisticated hunting weapons.

Descendants of the Thules are recognized as the ancestors of today's Inuit, a rich culture that grew out of a snow-covered land. The importance of snow is shown in their tools as well as their language. Just as southern people have many words to describe common items such as automobiles, Inuit have many words for different types of snow.

qanik (falling snow), qanittaq (new-fallen snow), aputi (snow on the ground), maujaq (soft snow on the ground), masak (wet falling snow), matsaaq (half-melted snow on the ground), aqilluqaaq (drift of soft snow), sitilluqaq (drift of hard snow), qirsuqaaq (refrozen snow), kavirisirlaq (snow rendered rough by rain and freezing), pukak (crystalline snow on the ground), minguliq (fine coat of powdered snow), natiruvaaq (fine snow carried by the wind), piirturiniq (thin coat of soft snow on an object), qiqurnaaq (snow whose surface is frozen), katakartanaq (hard crust of snow giving way under footsteps), aumannaq (snow ready to melt on the ground), aniu (snow for making water), sirmiq (melting snow used as cement for the snow house), isiriartaq (yellow or reddish falling snow), kinirtaq (damp, compact snow), mannguq (melting snow), qannialaaq (light falling snow), qanniapaluk (very light falling snow in still air)

*From **Arctic Languages**, edited by D. Collis, UNESCO 1990, p. 205

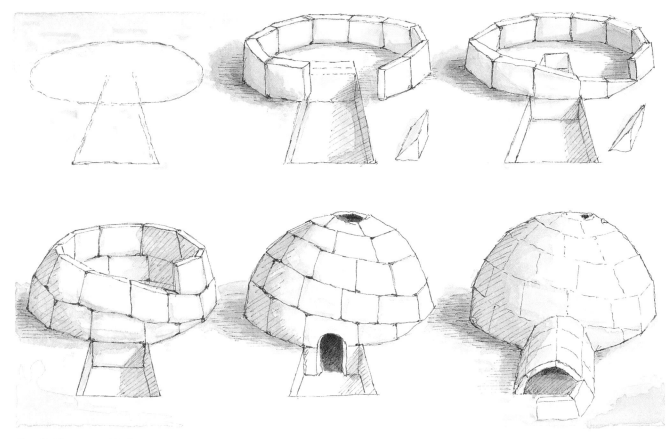

Building an Igloo

Step One: The outline of the planned igloo is marked in the snow, complete with entry tunnel.

Step Two: The first slabs of snow are cut from the tunnel area. Each slab is up to one metre (3 ft.) long, 30 to 60 centimetres (1-2 ft.) high and 15 centimetres (6 in.) thick. The slabs are slightly curved to accommodate the igloo's circular shape. The bottom layer is set into place. The first block, cut as a diagonal to allow for its easy removal from the snowbank, is discarded.

Step Three: The first few foundation blocks are cut diagonally so that the next level of block will rise with a slight spiral. The sides of each individual block are bevelled (giving them a trapezoid shape) so that it locks against its neighbour.

Step Four: The wall rises into a dome for maximum strength. Blocks are cut from within the igloo's outline. About 40 will be used. Some snow is left inside for use as benches.

Step Five: The walls rise to 2.5 metres (8 ft.).

Step Six: The entry tunnel, located on the south side away from the wind, is added. Cracks between blocks are packed tightly with snow, and a smoke hole is cut into the top.

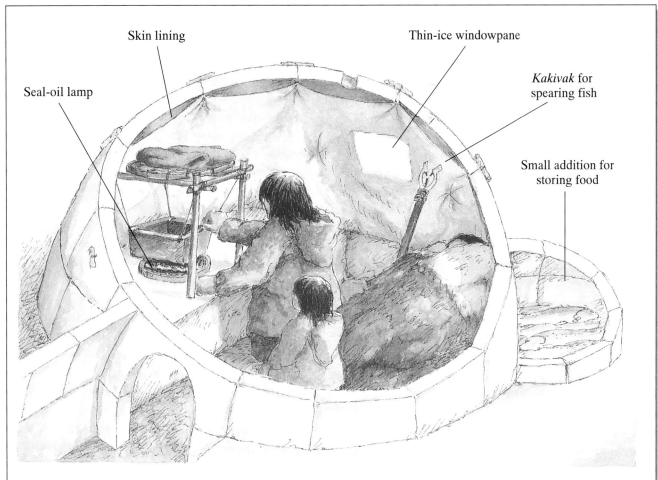

Skin lining

Thin-ice windowpane

Seal-oil lamp

Kakivak for spearing fish

Small addition for storing food

Life in an igloo

The Inuit word *iglu*, or igloo, really means any kind of house, but early visitors from the South assumed it meant snow house. Igloos built for families were quite well equipped and could last for several months.

Because of the snow's insulation value, igloos kept the inhabitants warm by blocking out cold air and trapping body heat inside. Even without a fire, they were about 18 degrees C (65°F) warmer than outside temperatures. A skin lining was often used so that the igloo could be kept warmer without melting the walls. Small seal-oil lamps provided light and heat.

The floor was snow, as were the large shelves used for cooking and sleeping. A block of snow near the door could be melted for drinking water, and food was kept in a small addition on the outside of the igloo, where it was refrigerated and safe from animals.

ANIMALS IN THE SNOW

Snow presents two main problems to animals: it is hard to travel through, and it covers up much of their food.

Many small animals like mice use the snow for shelter, building tunnels that will protect them from both the cold and their enemies. This, however, means that in winter, the snowy owl cannot find many rodents to eat, so it turns its attention to prey that cannot hide so easily. Suddenly, just because there is snow on the ground, the snowshoe hare finds itself on the owl's grocery list.

Fortunately, the hare has two tricks of its own. Each winter, its brown fur coat turns white, making it easier to hide in the snowy forest. And its oversize feet allow it to run quickly enough on top of crusty snow to avoid becoming Hare MacNuggets. But even with these two great defences, about 4 out of 10 snowshoe hares are eaten every winter.

Scientists classify northern animals into three groups: *chionophobes* cannot adapt to snow at all; *chioneuphores* manage to survive winters; and *chionophiles* need snow to live. As chionophiles (*chion* is Greek for snow), polar bears eat well all winter, sneaking up on seals that probably mistake them for snowdrifts. Without snow, polar bears and other chionophiles would die out.

Some chioneuphores must adapt to snow conditions each winter (adjusting their diet, getting white coats for camouflage, storing food, and so on), while others have evolved permanent characteristics. The long legs of moose and large hooves of caribou make winter travel possible; smaller animals like lynx and wolves make their daily travels easier by "ploughing" networks of trails through deep snow. Perhaps the simplest approach is taken by the grizzly bear: after eating heavily in the fall, it hibernates until the snow melts, when it can return to its routine.

Snow holds no hope for chionophobes, however, and these species simply leave for warmer places or face certain death.

Finding Food in Snow

When deep snow covers the ground, animals have two choices: they can stay and adjust to the wintry problem or move away to a place where snow is not such a hindrance.

While many birds fly south, spruce grouse and a few other ground-dwelling birds simply change their feeding habits. They head up into the trees for the season, where they can feed on berries and buds. The grouse only descends from the trees when it needs a rest, fluttering down into a snowdrift to carve out a cozy nest.

In the North, caribou and reindeer migrate long distances, leaving snowy mountain regions for sheltered valleys, where food is easier to find.

But the musk ox neither migrates nor changes its eating habits. It stays on the flat tundra, protected from the cold and snow by its thick, shaggy coat. It eats grass all winter, relying on the wind to keep the snow from becoming too deep. If the snow is too crusty for digging with its hooves, it smashes the ground with its heavy horned head until some edible plants are exposed.

Fight or Flight

The broader an animal's foot, the more easily it can support the weight of its body on top of the snow. Wolves have relatively small paws, making it hard for them to travel on snow, and the animals they hunt plan their defences accordingly.

Caribou, with their wide hooves, travel on top of snow fairly well and can escape by heading into deep snowdrifts. Moose, with smaller hooves, have little advantage over wolves in deep snow, so they tend to stand their ground and fight.

Deer, which have small hooves, pack down trails through their territory all winter long so that they can try to outrun attackers when necessary. They may jump over deep drifts if wolves are getting too close but risk becoming bogged down in a drift if they can't get back to their trails quickly.

Snow Boots

While snowshoe hares have large feet all year round, the feet of the willow ptarmigan, a ground-dwelling arctic bird, grow wider and longer each fall. The middle toe becomes longer, and feathers emerge all around the toes, creating a snowshoe that reduces the pressure of its footsteps by over 60 percent.

Similarly, caribou grow extra hair inside their hooves, making snow travel easier.

Life Below the Surface

While deep snow causes problems for many animals, it actually makes life easier for some small rodents. By building a network of tunnels in snowdrifts, the meadow vole can hide from its enemies all winter in dens that insulate it from cold temperatures. It can store food or eat the plant stalks left from autumn. Tall grasses provide the tunnels with a food supply, air shafts for ventilation and a route to different levels. The tunnels are dark, and surface sounds are muffled, but the snow cover keeps the temperature in the tunnels near the freezing mark, no matter how cold it is outside. Snowmobiles can crush a tunnel, but midwinter thaws are more dangerous, leaving animals unprotected before winter is over.

An animal built for snow

The bodies of animals have evolved in many different ways to increase their chances of surviving a snowy winter: hooves make it easier to dig through snow for food, large feet make travel over deep snow possible, and white coats help camouflage animals from their enemies. The long-eared spotted snow scooter is an imaginary animal that has been given many useful features for living in a snowy environment.

If such a bizarre beast did exist, it would no doubt thrive all winter but perhaps would not do as well in warmer seasons.

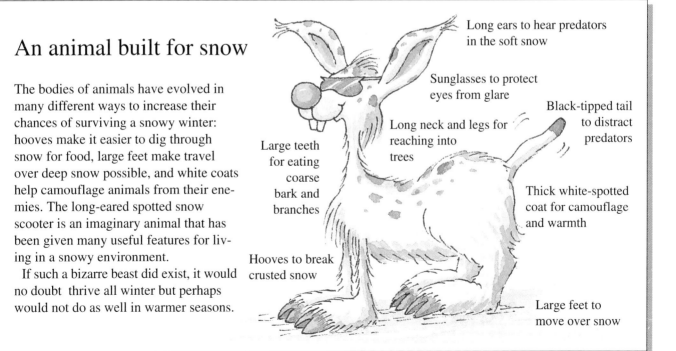

Long ears to hear predators in the soft snow

Sunglasses to protect eyes from glare

Black-tipped tail to distract predators

Long neck and legs for reaching into trees

Large teeth for eating coarse bark and branches

Thick white-spotted coat for camouflage and warmth

Hooves to break crusted snow

Large feet to move over snow

TRACKS IN THE SNOW

It is impossible to travel across snow without leaving tracks. And, when carefully examined, those tracks often tell fascinating stories about the animal or person who made them. But sometimes, they can be confusing and can lead to arguments that go on for years and years.

The most controversial set of tracks in the snow was photographed in 1951 during a British expedition to Mount Everest, in Nepal. Two of Britain's leading mountaineers discovered a series of footprints in the snow that measured 45 centimetres (18 in.) long and 33 centimetres (13 in.) wide. Their photographs of the giant footprints fuelled a debate that still rages four decades later. Ignoring the fact that the local Sherpas had called it Yeti for centuries, sensational newspaper headlines named the mystery beast which made the prints "the Abominable Snowman."

On the other side of the world, North Americans have Bigfoot, an animal named for the size of its tracks. While Nepal has few inhabitants and Yeti tracks are rarely seen, Bigfoot has been exposed to a much larger population. Since its tracks were first spotted in 1811, several people have seen glimpses of it and found traces of its tracks.

As the Yeti has proved, tracks in the snow can lead to interesting speculation, but amateur trackers should consider all the available clues. The shape of a footprint is important but so, too, is the pattern of the tracks, which can indicate how the animal moves its legs as it travels. Other important clues are those from the surrounding countryside that allow a tracker to narrow down the possibilities by ruling out animals which do not belong in that particular place.

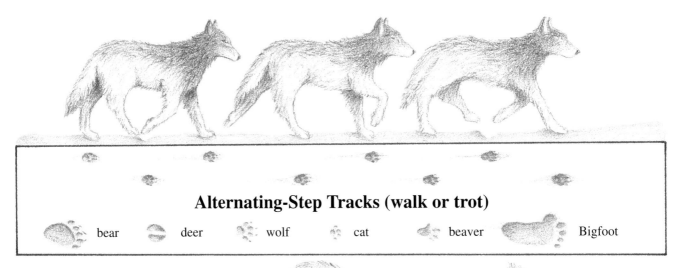

Alternating-Step Tracks (walk or trot)

bear   deer   wolf   cat   beaver   Bigfoot

The Track Patterns

1. Alternating-Step Tracks: This pattern is made by an animal which places its hind feet into the holes made by its forefeet, creating an alternating pattern that resembles the pattern of footprints people leave. Members of this group include wolves, deer, cats, beavers, porcupines, skunks and ground birds, like partridges.

2. Dual-Print Tracks: In deep snow, squirrels and other animals that bound forward two feet at a time leave footprints in pairs, as do mice and voles. As raccoons walk, they leave pairs of prints consisting of a hind foot next to a forefoot. Tree-perching birds also leave a double track as they hop forward with their feet parallel.

3. Quad-Print Tracks: In shallow snow, rabbits and squirrels leave four distinct prints as they bound along (in deep snow, the prints tend to blend together). They land on their forefeet, then bring their hind legs ahead of the front paws before launching into the next stride. Loping dogs also leave tracks in groups of four.

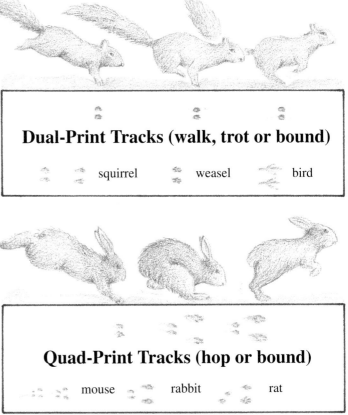

Dual-Print Tracks (walk, trot or bound)

squirrel   weasel   bird

Quad-Print Tracks (hop or bound)

mouse   rabbit   rat

The Habitat

To identify tracks correctly, it is important to examine the local habitat carefully. By limiting the list of "suspects" to the animals that inhabit an area, a good tracker can reach a conclusion much more easily. Cat tracks in a suburban backyard are more likely those of a domestic cat than of a mountain lion. A track that begins near a tree and ends abruptly is probably that of a bird which flew down from a branch to search for food before flying away. The more a tracker knows about animal habits and habitat, the easier the task will be.

The Track

After considering the track pattern and habitat, a good tracker will carefully examine the shape, size and depth of a track. A clear track in shallow snow may be crisp enough to outline the shape of hooves and claws, but deeper, soft snow does not leave a clear impression. Sunlight can cause problems as it melts snow around a print and enlarges it. Good clues can come from the depth of a print (deep prints mean a heavy animal) and the distance between prints (prints that are farther apart mean long legs or big jumps).

A monstrous rescue

Some people have "found" tracks of an Abominable Snowman, and a few others have "seen" the beasts at a distance in the Himalaya Mountains. But a curator of Calcutta's famous Victoria Memorial museum claimed to have lived with one for several days.

Captain d'Auvergne told colleagues that he had hurt himself while travelling through the mountains alone in 1938 and was in danger of dying of exposure. Cold, hungry and almost snow-blind, d'Auvergne claimed that he was found by a Yeti and carried several kilometres to a cave, where it cared for him until he was strong enough to travel again. His rescuer was almost three metres (10 ft.) tall, quite strong and intelligent enough to recognize his plight and help him.

Theories at the time suggested that this amazing beast was a survivor of a prehistoric race called the A-o-re people who had migrated to the upper reaches of the mountains and evolved into gigantic beasts. Capable of surviving bitter cold and high altitudes, they have rarely been seen and could be the key to the Yeti mystery.

SNOW FLURRIES

Snow Art: Olaus Magnus, the Archbishop of Upp-sala, Sweden, made the first attempt at portraying snowflakes with a series of woodcuts in 1555. However, they were so clumsily done that only one bears even the slightest resemblance to a flake.

Snow Caps: Mount Kilimanjaro, just 330 kilo-metres (200 mi.) south of the Equator, has a per-manent glacier on one of its three summits.

Snow to Water: Generally, snow has a volume 10 times that of water (10 buckets of snow would produce one bucket of water). That ratio can range from 6:1 for wet snow to 30:1 for dry snow.

Warming the Arctic: If all of its snow and ice were removed, the Arctic would be a much warmer place to live. The average annual temperature would rise by 15 Celsius degrees (27 F degrees).

The Snow Eater: In Alberta, warm winds called chinooks blow through Crowsnest Pass in the Rockies about 30 times a winter, raising tempera-tures by as much as 20 Celsius degrees (36 F degrees) in an hour.

Tracks of Giants: Using sonar, scientists can de-tect the trails of enormous icebergs whose bottoms scraped along the ocean floor thousands of years ago. Some of these trenches measure over two metres (6½ ft.) deep and 50 metres (164 ft.) wide.

Pumped Up: A freshly fallen dry layer of snow can be 97 percent air.

Moon Glow: A halo around a winter moon is a sign of impending snow. The ring effect is caused by ice crystals high in the air bending the moon's reflected light.

Snow Count: It has been estimated that during a 10-hour storm, one thousand trillion snowflakes will fall on a half-hectare (1 acre) plot.

Crop Predictions: Farmers in the last century had good reason for believing that "a year of snow would be a year of plenty." Heavy snow cover usually protected annual plants and winter grains from cold temperatures, keeping them healthy for the upcoming growing season.

Bad Timing: A mini ice age that lasted about 150 years wreaked havoc on the 18th-century Arctic explorers searching for the Northwest Passage to the Orient. Volcanic dust blocked enough sunlight to disrupt the amount of heat reaching Earth.

Mathematical Observations: Johannes Kepler, a mathematician, wrote a treatise in 1611 which stated that all snowflakes were six-sided. This first recorded scientific observation of snow triggered serious study of ice crystals and their connection to weather.

Snow Cover: Twenty-three percent of the planet — 50 percent of the land and 10 percent of the water — is under snow and ice for part of each year.

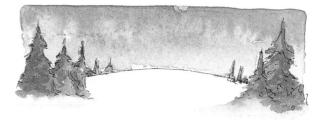

That's Not Fire, It's Snow: On overcast winter nights in dark parts of the country, a reddish light can sometimes be seen on the southwest horizon. Snowstorms often follow. One explanation is that turbulence in clouds unites oppositely charged water droplets, giving off an electrical discharge.

Falling Snow: The speed of a flake of falling snow is 3.5 to 6 kilometres per hour (2-3½ mph). Avalanches travel 330 kilometres per hour (200 mph).

Snow Throw: A popular game played by American native people involved throwing a "snow snake" — skimming a straight stick across smooth snow. The winner's stick went farthest.

Snow Cruiser: Designed by Dr. Thomas Charles Poulter and his staff at a cost of $150,000, this unusual craft was over 16 metres (55 ft.) long. Equipped with living quarters and a galley, it also contained a scientific laboratory, a darkroom and a machine shop. Its maiden voyage took place October 22, 1939.

The Year With No Summer: In 1816, dust from a volcanic eruption on Mount Tambora, in Indonesia, blocked solar radiation and totally disrupted normal weather patterns. In New England, there were frosts during the summer months and several centimetres of snow fell in early June.

Snow Clubs: The Montreal Snowshoe Club was formed in 1840 by 12 residents who enjoyed Saturday-afternoon jaunts through the countryside. Other clubs were formed, and soon races — including the high hurdles — were being held.

Snow Fakes: On November 13, 1946, Vincent Joseph Schaefer became the first person to produce artificial snow from a natural cloud. Flying a plane over Mount Greylock, Massachusetts, Schaefer scattered dry-ice pellets from an altitude of about 4,200 metres (14,000 ft.). Because of the unusually dry conditions, however, the snow evaporated before it hit the ground.

Laying It on Thick: It has been estimated that if all the ice in Greenland were spread evenly around the globe, the entire Earth would be coated with a frosting of ice five metres (17 ft.) thick.

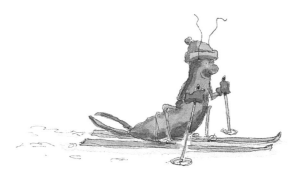

Winter-Hardy Bugs: The snow flea, found by the thousands atop snow on sunny winter days in Ontario and the eastern United States, is not really a flea. It is a springtail and can jump 60 times its miniature height.

Snow White: The surface of a fresh snow cover is composed of billions of tiny, randomly placed snow crystals. Each of these crystals acts as a microscopic mirror, reflecting up to 87 percent of all surrounding light.

Big Snow: America's biggest one-day snowfall was 193 centimetres (76 in.) in Silver Lake, Colorado, April 15, 1921. Canada's biggest in a day was 118 centimetres (47 in.) at Lakelse Lake, British Columbia, January 17, 1974.

Average Big Snow: America's snowiest place is Rainer Paradise, Washington, with an average annual snowfall of 1,460 centimetres (575 in.). Canada's highest annual snowfall is on Mount Fidelity, British Columbia, with an average of 1,433 centimetres (564 in.).

Business Sense: The world's first snowshoe factory opened in 1862 in Norway, Maine.

INDEX

When we thought of creating this book, our expertise on the subject of snow was pretty much limited to snowball fights and Sunday-morning toboggan runs at a local golf course. Luckily, we had some good resource people to help us out.

Our deepest gratitude goes out to Laurel Aziz, a thorough researcher who never complained about our slow start and missed deadlines, copy editor Susan Dickinson and proofreader Catherine DeLury.

Our families' ideas and patience were also invaluable throughout the project, as they are with all of our books. Special thanks go to Hayley, Jessica, Kristen, Sacha, Scott, Marg and Susan.